Apostrophes VIII

Apostrophes VIII

Nothing Is But You and I

E.D. Blodgett

UNIVERSITY *of* **ALBERTA** PRESS

Published by

The University of Alberta Press
Ring House 2
Edmonton, Alberta, Canada T6G 2E1
www.uap.ualberta.ca

Library and Archives Canada Cataloguing in Publication
Blodgett, E.D., author
        Apostrophes VIII : nothing is but you and I / E.D.
Blodgett.

(Robert Kroetsch series)
Poems.
Issued in print and electronic formats.
ISBN 978-1-77212-451-4 (softcover).—
ISBN 978-1-77212-458-3 (EPUB).—
ISBN 978-1-77212-459-0 (Kindle).—
ISBN 978-1-77212-460-6 (PDF)

        I. Title. II. Title: Apostrophes eight. III. Title: Apostrophes 8. IV. Title: Nothing is but you and I.

PS8553.L56A668 2019   C811'.54   C2018-906121-9
                                                                                    C2018-906122-7

First edition, first printing, 2019.
First printed and bound in Canada by Houghton Boston Printers, Saskatoon, Saskatchewan.
Copyediting and proofreading by Peter Midgley.

A volume in the Robert Kroetsch Series.

University of Alberta Press gratefully acknowledges the support received for its publishing program from the
Government of Canada, the Canada Council for the Arts, and the Government of Alberta through the Alberta
Media Fund.

Canada

Canada Council   Conseil des Arts
for the Arts   du Canada

Government

Tibi

Nichts ist als ich und du; und wenn wir zwei nicht sein,
So ist Gott nicht mehr Gott und fällt der Himmel ein.
—Angelus Silesius

[Nothing is but you and I; and if we two were not,
Then is God no more God and heaven would be naught.]

Contents

Water

Certain rains there are that do not seem to fall, but those are rains
that are exhalations of the air, and when you enter them,
your face is laid over with rain as if it were another skin
upon you, and more familiar than what is always there, and if
you were to touch it, it would not be the skin you know, the skin that holds
you as you are, but something larger that is yours and mine and all
that stands mute around us—the trees that have grown fuller, the earth beneath
our feet, flowing with the air. What is there, then, around you that

is not given of the air, unnoticed and departing with
the rain? Perhaps, you will say, that such small rains, that make the air
appear green, but green breathing, are only verdant air, and all
that comes before us as leaf and grass, and as you speak, you touch your face
with hands that have also been touched by rain: how to tell whose skin
this is, that is the breath of everything, where birds are always at rest?
So it is that we are walking through a sea of air, the rain upon
us and taken in as we inhale, the rain that lies almost

asleep upon the trees. Perhaps birds do not fly but swim,
and we are kin to whales moving through their deeper continents
and carried just as the moon would have them move unresisting through
unfathomable space, their fate not theirs alone but shared with us
where we, not always knowing, breathe the immeasurable rain
that shapes itself through all that it moves toward, taking the form of stone,
your face and its several contours that hold and then become
the rain and its slow infinities flowing out of air.

Trieste

Someone in the winter darkness said the word *Trieste*, and
the air around it parted as if it were a bell sounding in
a fog, no one certain where the sound was coming from, but all
of it, each mournful note that weighed upon each syllable,
sank into us, but not as stones or stricken birds, nor war that is
always approaching, no, it sank as if it were an echo that
was on the way of coming back to where it had begun, before
it lost its way, falling apart in fragments, lying on our bones
like shells upon a distant beach through which the small waves retreat
and leave behind a clatter of skulls that try to laugh not knowing how.

Give me your hand, there is no other way of getting through that strange
music rising through the afternoon, and as we make our way
through unfamiliar streets, it seems as if we must step over it,
the rattle of the sea invisible around our feet, and in
the doorways voices murmur constantly, calling in tongues that are
unknown to us, but doorways that are empty, not a single child
in sight, no higher notes of ecstasy that through the boulevards
pierce the air strewn with shade, only the backwash of the sea
to guide us toward places that cannot be found—perhaps the house
that saw your mother's birth is just beside us or the churches or—

and each of us is on the point of asking how to reach the place
of where things began, a page declaring what the heroine is called
and how she chose to dress, how colourful the sight of soldiers in
the streets, the harboured ships, when rituals of empire lingered here,
and children were not dreamt of but without the slightest summons poured
everywhere through the streets, and flowers in the trees above their heads
declared it to be spring before departing with the ships, their wakes
the last sounds across the bay, or memories of wakes that no
one on the quay can fail to hear or think to hear, and if you ask
if it is here or here, you will be given these receding echoes that

are hidden in the voices, murmuring unbidden and without
imparting sense. How to compose beginnings here, merely to
conceive of genesis, where only the sea speaks, and speaking fills
the spaces of the soul with cries too intimate to take the shape
of words, but there Trieste all alone resides, invisible
but carried everywhere, winter shadows helplessly at play
upon its walls, impossible to say where wall and shadow end,
and our shadows with them entering us? So evening falls,
the difference that we thought we knew, of flesh and air, the darkness and
the disappearing sun, uncertain, birth no other than an end.

Glass

Sometimes when you speak, it seems as if your voice had been engraved
into clear glass, and into darkness, against all absence, it
bears the light before it undeterred and each syllable
that spills into the air, whatever word takes shape, the light that just
the sun gives up is altered so that pebbles, should you speak of them,
emerge against the ground as moments after rain, the sun come back
again, the light leaping from them. How could God have known, when he

commanded light to be, that light was not the merest presence of
the stars and all the objects of the world appearing in the sun,
that light is not darkness denied, a dance in time that steps and stops,
that light is that preface invisible preceding all that is,
incarnate in each leaf and blade of grass that pass into your voice,
edges of light you might say that glance off each other, as
of light floating in a moving mirror, clear as bells of glass?

Shells

Solitudes of birds come down about you in the shape of shells,
the casual immortality of what they left behind carved
upon a rock, and in the falling light, the surface of the rock,
the shells, as if they never were, give way, unable to resist
the water moving without effort everywhere around them, the
echo of it barely to be heard, an echo breathing through
the thin light, the rock, the shells, the passage of the birds that leave
nothing behind but shadows, not of wings but merely of the air

that momentarily unfolds and then returns to what it was,
a world dissolving into something without name, and on the shore
we pause, unable in the going away to know if what remains
is what had been. Perhaps shades that seem to rise and overtake
the sun are shades of other shades that come and go across the air,
each cast from other shades, their breath passing over stone
as other water that is made of air that, lifting the shape of things,
takes the world back, all reflection reversed into itself.

Questions

Race is not a colour, black and white, that like a finished thought
stands resolute before our eyes, for how could we invent, you ask,
mandalas that composed of black and white are seen lying content
in one eternal embrace, and in them eyes of their own that gaze back
at us, each of the eyes opposed but calling to the other, each
unable to come into being if the other disappeared?
It's possible that race is just a room where you and I unknown

to one another enter. Darkness settles over us as if
only air were capable of blessing the things that fill the world,
the chairs merely shadows, ivory figures that shimmer with
a greater beauty after dark, and should I touch you, how could I
tell what aspect of the twilight moved beneath my fingers, no
distinction possible? Race, my friend, is that moment when
light too sudden fills the room and everything about us is

without the least warning left naked, familiarity
of fragments that cannot discover where they used to be, the whole
that held them gone. How to put words together again, to make
the simplest order where embracing is denied, eternity
reduced to shards of things unseen before that fall at random from
an incandescent sky where birds refuse to fly, the parts of us
remaining moving through the dust every trace erased, and what

would there be left of you, and how could I without temerity
say *I*, nothing there that would respond, and what of beauty, mind
and passion, one by one so ruined that no light might find
the shape they held, and might it be that even the sun that was once
where you and I had stood before each other, happy in the play
of light and shade, is our sun no more but light that burns without
pity over the world, you and I, a wake invisible?

A Woman Sitting

An old woman sitting in the sunlight, birds that seem to turn
in aimless circles in the light above her head, birds that seem
to be birds that float and fall and sometimes disappear but not
into the distance but somewhere close where in their absence they
could be touched going past, where traces of themselves were left,
a gift that settles in the mind like dust too fine to notice, just
its passing over time, departures that linger so long that you

cannot remember if they left at all. The woman on the bench
seems to have fallen asleep, unable to follow all the turns the birds
have taken falling into absence, a smile floating on her face
as if knowledge of the birds was what had made her smile, and as
one by one they take their leave her smile floats with them into
the air where only what has been or may have been appears to pause,
all floating there in one eternal turn, the air itself

fallen asleep and breath become a solitary bird that comes
and goes at random. Who can say what it is her face resembles in
the sleeping air, its smile departing with the birds? Perhaps it is
how oceans in the dark appear to someone passing thoughtless on
the shore, almost invisible but so full of silence you
might think God was somewhere underneath the waves consumed
by all that might have been and one old woman nearly walking there.

Winter's Night

The shadows are so clear across the snow beneath the moon that you
would think that they could be no other than the souls of those who walked
beside them, breathless souls that had decided to lie down beneath the night,
and while their bodies walked slowly toward a house that stood against
the far horizon, they, longing for the light to bring them into the world,
stretched forth upon the snow, the surface of it blown shapeless from
the wind, begin to know the clean aurora of the cold upon
the emptiness of what they were, and were it possible, they would

have cried out with that surprise of those who stumble on the sea
with no idea of what it is that lies beneath their feet, and they
are overcome, their one desire to be the sea, to move without
the weight of bodies over water through the space that separates
the day from night, to hold distance unthinking in their hands as one
might hold the whole sea and all the creatures that are what it is
inside, and all of them like figures on snow moving slowly toward
the light, their souls like new birds suddenly aware of wings.

Palestine

Beyond all hearing, as snow during the night it began
to fall, no one waking, night enfolding you and everyone,
too deep for any to resist, and fell as small pieces of flesh.
No animal could walk so softly through the night, their feet against
the ground as if they were not moving at all, and all passing by
as creatures whose presence was beyond measure. But it was not
the snow that moved through the air, but children or what was left

of them, delicate, small hands that if one were held in yours,
you would not think it was a hand but rather roses falling past,
feet that had been running moments before, and now of all feet
it was their memory of running that was falling, eyes that had
been so full of sunsets over the sea were now sunsets that
were falling into disappearing seas, the lovely whorls of ears
that carried music into their frail bones, the air an echo whose

only sound was white and something like snow that takes you by
surprise, a snow that if you knew it was so near and falling on
familiar grass, you would be moved to comfort, taking all of it—
roses, music, seas that are not seen again, the feet that are
whiteness itself—into your hands to carry it into your waking
where, after all the children have fallen where they could not help
but fall, they follow stars that have gone out as if they had not been.

Skating

As if it were an old painting slowly coming to mind across
the winter light of afternoon, and we, like tired hunters came
around a hill, and starting to descend began to see the rest
of it, the black streaks of birds in the sky that had eluded us
throughout the day, but birds that we were now happy to give up,
and yet how strange these birds that did not seem to fly, their wings spread out
upon the clarity of heaven—: this, we thought, must be the shape
that ecstasy must take in flight. And then we saw the trees stand up

upon the hills, and looking down across the snow, we saw a pond
and on the pond figures that may have been hunters once like us,
and each of them struck the pose they most desired as birds might
if they were caught the moment that the sun had seized them, holding them
an instant for stars to see when night began to fall across the hill
and trees and pond, each of the skaters in their solitary turns
knowing this is why they trace eternal circles through the slow
light of afternoon, counterfeiting planets, immortal birds.

Aubade

Deeper through the woods the early light was lying on the branches,
nothing quite awake, the moon uncertain of its light, the air
sleepy with the songs of birds that are forgotten as soon as they begin,
and half-awake you grasped my hand in yours, your fingers curling around
one of mine unable to be sure of where they were as if
the dream that still lay over them had not quite reached an end, and you
were not upon a bed but given up to an infinity
where darkness was the only thought that moved between the stars and you,

and if another sprang into that space, a thought where suns might rise
above familiar trees, it was not known, and so your fingers as
smaller birds, forgotten where they are in darkness infinite,
will grasp whatever else is near, astray and unremembered, without
the barest light among the trees. And so your hand in flight from all
the dark entering everywhere fell blindly next to mine, and clung
upon it, nothing else within the air, the darkness holding you
and you holding me, a solitary branch in early light.

Arriving

There are old men who wait nightly in unlit rooms waiting for you
to come out of the light to them, their hands stretching forth to greet
your slow arrival. What will you say as you enter the room where all
the friends that you have passed beside from childhood, from years of high
spirit when everything was possible until you stood upon
the threshold of your most ancient age when light seemed almost dark,
and those who had gone on before appeared to sit beside you in
the shade awhile, and you might speak to them not knowing what they might

have answered? But now approaching those old men through rooms that never see
the light, you see that they are not the men you thought they were but mere
shades of men that sing through the dark, and one was singing what
the soul might be, another how the air was opened by the first
of butterflies, another sang almost inaudibly about
the gods, whether they were or where, and all the singing flowed into
a single chant in which the voices came and went. So it was
that nothing stood before you but the dark that filled itself with all

that could be known, and there was room for all that was unknown, and it,
more softly than the other voices sang in that place where all
perspectives disappear, asking what the sense of pebbles is
or why children lose their way and are forgotten. Into this
you make your way, hearing singing everywhere, but singing that
sings without the need for words, and if there is eternity,
what would it be but knowing that is not the knowing that we know—

birds in early spring belong to it, flying without the least
awareness through it, brief eternities in every note that falls
away from them invisible and then returning as a sudden shower
of snow might disappear to that absence where all snow springs forth,
descending past the stars, and holding in its fall whatever sings
white and what the white might be—this is what you approach, and like
birds your voice beginning to cast forth an innocence it could
not know that it possessed, gazing at old men in dark rooms.

Hand

It was a moment when the light was most pure, before dawn,
without the mediation of the sun, the stars invisible,
and you were standing inside the light, left beside a road that stretched
unerringly across infinity and stone, without a tree
where birds might perch, absence falling from their eyes undeterred,
nothing else to see but you unmoving there with pebbles at
your feet, upright against a sky that was no more than pure light

that lifted where sight could not pursue it. What are you to do,
a threadbare solitude your sole adornment, and if you were aware
of it, it was not knowledge that was yours—: these are landscapes where
hypotheses do not arise, and all that gathers shape within
the mind has no before or after, and you against it like a stick
so thin upon the plain that should a sun pass over you, you could
not cast a shadow on the ground, the pebbles glowing whitely at

your feet. Where then without the sun and stars does all the light come from
if not the eyes that open in your face as you and I come in
to sight, where other suns are turning slowly there? And light was all
you had to say, the meaning of it something that slipped over us,
a second skin, the one horizon that we shared where solitude
seemed to disappear, the pebbles at your feet beneath us both,
our hands one hand upon the air, a gift given of the light.

Lost

The late sun falls slowly into the afternoon of your eyes, and there
it pauses as one might pause to take a breath, to find exactly where
the trees are standing, how the land descends, and where the stream is on
the point of disappearing under the hill where all light goes down
beside it, taking breath and sight away, nothing left to wait
for but the possibility of stars that may on the breathless sill
of afternoon begin to rise. This is almost to be lost,

to find oneself in darkness, light removed, all of it gone into
the silence where your eyes had been, and in its place the absence of
the shape that waiting takes, the trees where they have always been inside
the silence. But if all were gone, no one would conceive the stars,
and if they rose, they would not seem to be stars, but something in
the dark that makes it darker still, the light that haunts the blind when they
remember, after the sun has settled in their hearts, how stars were once

the only light that intermittent fell around them as a rain
for them, and flowers breathing with them in the dark of afternoons,
knowing that these were not the stars that everyone believes are stars,
but places where a universe begins before going out,
a particle of dust, perhaps as large as we might be if we
were seen by God in afternoons that are not ours to know, but just
in passing and unable to determine where, merely lost.

Creed

As one, lying in bed at night in some foreign city might
hear the sounds of familiar things rise up—the clock nearby that tolls
the early hours, a dog that barks its intermittent riffs of barks
that turn the air into fragments of solitude calling to mind
leaves as they dissolve to ash in summer fires, and farther away
a train that whistles to the absence, and still farther stars that fill
the silence—: none of this needs to be more than savoured, slowly and

without emerging from the dark and taking shape. Returning home
has sounds of such size, and as you walk through streets that you have known
so deeply every turn is seen without a glance, you gaze around
at everything in its unchanging twilight, lanes that wander off
into the dark, acacias on the boulevards, and then you turn
and all that was familiar seems to be but shades of what you knew,
the outlines fading, only the stars standing above in certainty.

Our creed must be the stars, collapsing, falling, turning through the night
where birds weave their way, their warp undetectable across
the space of soundless twilight, spirits of unfathomable air,
nothing in their wake. Of this creed, you said, they must be souls
that sing among themselves in notes pitched too high for us to hear,
unlike the birds that we have seen but more familiar, and each
gazing back at us, homing birds that sense landscapes of
something they have known, ghosts of ourselves, haunting us and stars.

Church

Above the bed we place a picture of a church. Above the church
not the slightest sign of birds that might have been turning in
the late afternoon, nor sun, nor clouds. But snow had fallen, roofs
had turned white with silence, the absence of the birds become a frame
for all the depths from which silence rises, as if silence were the tree
we did not see, a tree like those that placed all solitude
before our eyes, where people had walked idly by before

and then departed, leaving traces now invisible against
the fallen snow, walking into silence. Only the spire is left,
the church, a monastery and its domes. The windows are without
the least light. You might have thought that here everything concludes,
no pathway going toward it or away, no singing in the air,
where its almost forgotten stillness falls, another snow
that lies upon us in the night, silences in residence.

Thresholds

Were it possible, if destiny did not forbid, we might
be standing side by side, speaking on a threshold that could not
be known to us. What did we speak of if not of God and trees, of how
the sun will disappear, all of it turned to air, invisible
and unremembered? All that stays is how your voice returning stood
against the air, a sound of weathered stone. Perhaps it is the stone
that is the threshold of a heaven, and where, arriving, we do not
arrive but simply begin to wake, the going and the coming a

reaching into the dark, a way of speaking that would give a thought
to what appears to be its end, silence taking it away.
So it is to stand inside snow, without a sense of where
north might be, the destiny of stars removed, every turn
the same, the body that we think we are another silence that
becomes another echo of all silence, every word
white and falling through the white air. So it is that fate
has an end, and God, and we waken where all we might

have said stands around us flowered in eternal suns, the light
the single sentence of the world, no word evoking silence, no
conclusion of arrivals, just the light that spreads across stone,
all coming and all the going turns that turn upon themselves,
nothing to remember, all that is spoken gathering itself
into whatever is, and we are that stone, the threshold of
the heaven we imagined without seeing, light spreading on
the merest stone of us, wherever in darkness we happened to fall.

Prayers

What you may have said I do not know, but I, when I was on
the point of falling asleep, knelt upon the sill of silence and
the dark, and said a prayer that asked that those who stood around me would
be blessed. It was a way of staying longer here before the long
surrender fell, as birds against the twilight by the shore start
to make circles through the air before they settle for the night,
or, on the edge of autumn, longer flights farther out to sea

until it is only horizons visible, each of the birds
gone to where they go. You might have thought the words I spoke in prayer
were no more, passing over my lips, no more substantial than
the passage of birds that in their distances all appear alike:
none of the words of those nocturnal prayers have changed, the cadences
of each always reappearing familiar as rain, familiar
as birds almost out of sight, and all that we have now are not

the words but what they have left behind in us, remnants of
a *cantus firmus*, but whose sense is in the voice that murmurs on
the borders of the sea, the small waves that fall without fail
against your feet, and when I hear you unawares and speaking to
those whom you have lost, remnants rise in you, and you might say
that you have heard birds returning through your words, the sound that's in
their wings a music that remembers how it was that God could be.

Departure

Without warning you left, and if you turned, it was not clear—: you walked
just as you had always walked, steadily into what there was
for you to know, and in your wake gleanings lay unnoticed, small
illuminations, passages of stone and broken air, but where
we were to go was never sure, as if the rivers descending toward
the seas began to choose other ways to fall unforeseen,
the seas no longer the sole goal of all descending, but perhaps

beginnings that had not been known. And so things cannot be what
they seem to be, whole and indivisible, but are themselves
and something else, as if always waiting for some departure, some
insistence of a layer of dust upon a fallen wall or the
remains of birds after they have gone, a little song that hangs
longer than one had thought. And so it is that we are not what we
had thought we loved, but only how we loved, a certain way we turned

before moving away—*then* the dust that was invisible
lies against the light upon the fading walls, and songs take shape
ex nihilo, a nothing that cannot be but be—and then
all departure is a coming back, but not as ghosts that stand
uncertain in the dark, but just as flowers might, standing up
in all the colours they have chosen in the sun, bright upon
the mind, at any moment spring, a bird, the figured fall of rain.

Beaches

Beaches before anyone arrives exhale an air so pure
you would not think that anyone had walked beside their shores, the waves
so tranquil that the fish that swim beneath them seem lifted by
the ecstasy that saints alone possess, some beneath the shade
that trees bestow upon them, others in the first light the sun
sends tentatively forth upon the water and the shore. A bird
sings out invisible across the air, giving distance to

the sky. If statues could be seen from where they are inside where all
their silence gathers shape, the fish that pause where the sun comes to rest,
the singing air and distance in your eyes, so close it can be touched,
then the being that is only lent to us would seem ours,
and you might sing, another bird whose breathing is the air itself
that sings, and we, the utmost moment ours, exhale the stillness of
the air, the dream of fish unmoving in the sun gathering us.

Openings

Some things must be given up. Knowing the souls of trees is one
of these, and with their souls how they conceive salvation for themselves,
or is it that their souls, the breath eternal they exchange among
each other is without the slightest origin, as if you had
entered a room where nothing that you saw was ever seen before
and all of it contained the sense that it possessed nothing that
belonged to it, but all of it exhaled an air of different hues,
and all of them—yellow, blue or red—flowed through each other, no

colour lasting more than instants before becoming another. Is
it but a river, was the thought that crossed your mind, whose water takes
up the sun in passing, flows beyond it, falling near its banks,
careless of what the light has done? Even to take it in your hands
would not bring nearer the souls of such creatures, their breath entering ours,
we becoming the room where they in breathing are, and can we tell
if we are waiting for them or they us, salvation unsought,
their breathing opening a universe where stars fall as rain?

Singer

Before the fall of dusk, outside the window where you lie, the last
of starlings sings, but not the song he sings as if for the last
time, when no leaf, no blade of grass is forgotten, each transformed
into evanescent riffs of melisma, none the same, the air
turned to music. At dusk and dimmer light, his music takes a shape
no one could have guessed, and you are on the point of asking if
this is the same bird, but the change is in the tone, softer and more
unconcerned, the intervals between them longer, as if he had

begun, like us, to listen to the silence made, and when
he sings, a tune comes back sometimes, enough that we can see that each
burst is no longer self-contained but of a longer song, yet in
each pause it seems he has begun to step back from the song, when there
was nothing in the morning to suggest the singer and the song
were not of one being, and so we wonder which is it of
the two that hesitates, the singer or the song, and how can it be
that this bird, that has no other life but to invent songs, can now

stand aside from them? No other gesture touches the heart so,
to know the silence shared, partly his and partly the song, to reach
the highest ranges possible and know the song is not his
but only placed into his keeping for the briefest moments, then
removed, and all the longer spaces in between are where his knowledge rests,
the music graver, tinged with sorrow never sung before, a kind
of waiting in it, neither the song nor the bird sure of what
the dark might bring, the music allowing each leaf its leafiness.

Sarabande

Fountains are enough, the water in the shape of dreams that have
not yet arrived. Here you might forever grow as slow as stones
that have no other thing to do but lie against the sun, wait
for rain or, if it were to happen, listen to the chatter of
the little birds, at last to be a tree, and where you stand your sole
companions would be wind, the river passing at your feet, your shade
spreading beneath the sun. Fountains are enough and children that,
too young to know that they are dreams, pass into the limpid air,

too swift to feel the tree that arches over them, unable to
return as birds invisible within the shade where all without
resistance falls—the sun, the water, and the shade—but falls as if
gravity were not necessity, falling as flowers at
the close of summer fall, their falling a withdrawal toward the sun
departing, going away without desire into a night that has
no end of dark, its darkness receding into deeper darkness where
flowers are the dream of fountains flowing at your feet unseen.

Dreamt

As those whom you have loved pass slowly away one by one,
something in you takes note, no name effaced, the shape of each
smile inscribed by some invisible and unerring hand,
nothing essential missed, but each so fleeting that often you ask
yourself if you have failed them or they have failed you, their coming back
uncertain as the sun in rainy countries, darkness where the trees
stand up unseen, the emptiness of air all that you breathe in,

so unlike the dreams that you are given, all of them who seemed
to have disappeared return, and what you think are dreams that you
might dream are those that you have loved who now dream you, but dream as trees
might dream in darkness, dreaming the world, and so, unresistant, you
fall asleep into the dream they have of you, their solitudes
all they have for you, seas of solitudes where underneath
the wind, you lie as driftwood, bare, uncompassed, dreamt inside the dark.

Stream

How filtered is the light that makes its way through old acacias, like
a stream that has nowhere to go but fold around a rock, move up
against a long spit of sand where birds process so stately that
you would consider it a royal moment, the lift and fall of feet
a dance that follows music that cannot be heard, but music that
is in them as a slow, eternal gift, a knowledge that is of
a cosmos, whole, incapable of change, a knowledge that when each

of them takes flight into the air as one they are the one bird
that is the deepest knowledge that possesses them. Behind them on
the sand the tracks that are their wake, the silent code of what they know,
their gift to us that is not given to be read, but simply seen,
perhaps remembered, waiting to disappear beneath the rain that will
wash them all into the stream flowing past the spit, the rock,
a knowledge of a cosmos that has nowhere to go in air distilled.

Disappearing

When the rain had gone, the earth exhaled—: you would not have thought I saw
you as you were another afternoon upon a chair that rose
above your head and all your bones had fallen deeper in your flesh,
more invisible than ever when you breathed, the light that fell
upon your face autumnal, memories of summer falling through
it straying briefly on your face before they disappear, children too far
to hear. I might have reached into the air as if the only joy

of fall were taking all of it in hand, the children that we were,
the summers and the light, and all of it would have spilled over, stars
that are always outside, the where of where they are unable to
be grasped, their brightness hidden in the sun and hidden in your bones.
Knowledge is not for us, content with rain. Whatever rises from
the darkness of the earth, taking it in without the slightest thought,
where it resumes in us. Its transience now ours, we stand up and look.

Temple

Gazing at the temple at Segesta, certain things at first
might be missed, so grandly does it dominate the field against
a fading sky, but everything that danced around its feet gave forth
summer at its fullest splendour—poppies where a mild breeze
passed, and other flowers that would have been daisies had they grown
here. And sitting on a bench were other gazers that one might
assume were you and me, intently looking at the temple and

its ancient columns holding up a frieze, the roof and walls spread out
upon the ground, their heap absorbed by distant hills, she who seems
so much like you—consider how she leans away from him, as if
the temple did not hold her gaze, nor any flower nor the hills,
but something no one sees but you, as if in that moment you
had seen a stillness that was so absolute you could not believe
it to be there at all, as if it were the air you saw, the air

that carried in itself the memory of all that had passed by,
its only trace the breeze among the flowers, jubilations now
dissolved, all the processions that had come and gone impossible
to bring to mind—the prayers, the movements that became a slow dance,
and our sitting here where we have never been, nothing in
our eyes but sacred stone, and if a god came by, how could we tell
him from the flowers and the hills, the breeze perhaps giving him up.

Tapestry

The evening light descending through the window pauses beside your face,
a little warmth still floating through its breath and bearing light from stars
that have not yet appeared, a light diffused and so at home inside
the dark they pass unnoticed but already turning round your face.
Or is it you that turns around the stars? Just the turning is all
it is, the centre darkness where you sit, the turning so slow
it does not seem to have the least motion, your eyes unfocussed and

gazing into to the dark. You might have been a portrait of yourself,
a portrait woven from the random threads of dark that fall across
your face, and woven from whatever passes through the night—the sound
of birds that leave a wake of wings behind, a rustle in the trees,
nothing to be seen except at play upon your face. Perhaps
a head gives up and lies upon your lap, as if you were she
who tamed the unicorn. How pensive has the darkness now become

making its way through you, the trees mere shadows, the birds the last
echo of the light. The room that holds you seems unable to
give up the weave of its eternity, the stars unable
to depart. Who remembers the clarity of things, exposures of
the sun, the naked solitudes of stones? What does your gaze
fall upon, the dark descending through your eyes, all that is
the falling stars coming and going into the night upon your face?

Winter Dreams

Sunset enthrals them, walking slowly on the shore, and gazing out
as far as they might see toward the mountains folded at the end
of sight, uncertain in the rising mist how they might feel if one
stretched out a hand to stroke them, the one anchor in the darkness that
begins to fall upon them, but they, the people drifting on the coast,
they are yet more enshrouded, nothing of the disappearing sun
upon them, their faces losing shape, and on the water birds rise up

almost without moving, calling through the twilight, as if it were
the water calling, making little songs of indecision, earth
itself speaking at random, speaking dusk, and suddenly you wished
to stand and answer, as you might rise within a dream, the ache of it
falling over you as just another dark might fall, unsure
of what to call for, uncertain who was dreaming, you or those who stand
upon a shore, music falling on their faces as the barest rain

might fall, their skin alive but now alive as if reborn as rain
and air and little songs that have nowhere to go, and they begin
to dream themselves incorporeal—not rain, but rain in its
effect, a rain of undiscovered, brief nostalgias, and not air,
but air so invisible it seems of all departures the most
irrevocable, the songs it carries carried forever away,
at home in you dreaming of the sun setting on the shore.

Eternities

Sitting in a garden, you were telling stories that began
without the least announcement, just a word that altered silence from
a rustle in the leaves surrounded by a stillness that might
have been the sound eternity would make if we were able to
take note of it, and in the play of leaf and possibility
your voice would hesitantly rise, as if afraid eternity
might be disturbed, your words stepping like those of children who have not
quite learned what walking is and forming steps that seem to move toward

things that no one can see, but in their slow unfolding standing up
in front of us as questions that are more like paths that move into
a twilight where the rustle of the leaves is all the answer that
comes back, but leaves that are suspended in eternities that are
at home inside the stories that you tell, stories with threads that weave
from one silence to another through the dark, the shape of what
you are in that unanswerable that you exhale, the air awake
with birds unseen before, each listening with timeless eyes.

Barely

Grandeur was not what you desired: the barest tree standing at
the corner, leaves mostly gone, the outline of a tree against
a sky in autumn, clouds behind, a sparrow scratching at its roots,
a street where people have gone on, no more familiarity
is needed but the silence that is everywhere, a slower sun
that passes almost invisible across a wall. Along such
a street you have walked, together or apart, unable to
recall how often—all that comes to mind is what the music is,

music that can only be at home in silences so bare
they need no more than mere transparency to cover them, and just
in patches so the silence and the music are unable to
be more than what they are, companions of the naked trees, the least
of sparrows, both barely touching, chiaroscuro music that
returns light to the sun, the silence singing as the smallest stone
might sing, barely heard, and for a moment not a stone, but called
into the light refrain that pauses on the trees, gravity gone.

Rooms

Like certain afternoons that seem incapable of going away,
the flowers unclosed that close without the presence of the sun, the sun
itself pausing across the sea, and nothing seeming to breathe, and yet
not breathless, everything wakefully at rest, the birds slower in
the skies, so every room is left after you have passed
through it, the air changed—an air that no one knows beginning to
offer up the memory of flowers that had stood around

you in another childhood of endless afternoons, a spring
that was the all of springs, beginnings of the bees, anemones
that leap from seas as fountains in the early suns. What more are we,
who are unable to be without their being what we breathe, that all
that is not all but all that is our knowing of what we cannot see,
the nearest of the grace that falls upon us in the lightest rain
through light that lingers, the rooms you walk through full, our being breath?

Herons

How your eyes are drawn to herons, their heads tucked under, standing on
the shore, their solitary dreams wrapping around their bodies, dreams
that are what we might think are feathers where the rain seems almost to
dissolve, returning to the air, where night without its darkness shies
away. No one but other dreamers—trees that line the bank, their kin
of pebbles motionless among their roots, the stream beneath them all
where everything that passes, you and I, lie down, mirrored and
unable to reply with gestures of their own—can fathom dreams

like these, dreams that have no waking here, that do not start against
the setting sun nor cease within the early light. What other dreams
are these but where eternity begins, eternity that is
not ours—that eternity that does not begin in any place
but moves unmoving as a breath of air filled with slow rain
about to fall, a rain that falling cannot be for us but for
divinity's delight, a rain immeasurable that is without
beginning or an end where herons seem to glide, their being rain?

Vodník

A willow weeping over water where we passed, and as you saw
it, what you saw was something like a veil and lace and glints of light
rising off the water woven into all you saw, a light
of water and the sun that floated in the air, the pond a part
of the tree and young leaves. We moved slowly off, a veil inside
us and the floating light, unable to see beyond the veil where a god
lay down to rest upon the light. And there he slept, his sleeping wide

awake, and in his eyes nothing that did not turn—the willow and
its veil, the rising pond, the leaves, and us and all his eyes might summon up
to pass in sight and disappear, all that rose there divine
desire, but seen from every side at once, as one might see from afar
and very near, seeing the tree but a tree in deepest thought, and through
the thought the sound of water in the light, and our walking there,
stepping inside the sleep a god might have, thinking us and light.

Frieze

It was a season cut from glass, of cautious birds, evening that
pauses in patches in the trees as if composed of memories
barely visible, and each fallen from a labyrinth
of stories to linger briefly here before the rising of the stars.
You see the thinness of it, its fragility, your eyes unsure
if all of it, the birds and stars, might have been spoken of in spells,
of spells adrift from larger tales and all unable to depart,

a season that has no way out and open in us like a frieze
where we begin to see ourselves in low relief, so delicate
that you might think that you are leaves of willows that have just begun
to give their softest green to air, and if a goddess were to be
needed, then this green were she, etched beside us in the air,
a melody of birds woven soundlessly into her hair,
all of us the merest echoes of a script without trace.

Pool

The night my father died, the stars emerged and gave the sky its shape,
moving slowly from east to west until horizons took them and
they disappeared, the silence of their passage falling over all
of us as if it were a passing of an early snow that drifts
but briefly through the dark. If we spoke, it was in passing, an
opening of silence, a little spring that surfaced from the ground
and fell away, the grass around it bending momentarily

toward the water never seen before. If that is what you were,
moving in the briefest of springs and passing on as water does,
your silence must have been the silence of a stream invisible
whose passage lies beneath the ground, rising beyond sight to form
a pool and then depart, a pool where frogs rise up and sing throughout
the night, as if they were the bearers of a message that cannot
be known, but passed alone between themselves and the reflected stars.

Fountain

At dusk it takes you by surprise, a turn into a garden that
you have never seen, and under trees the sound of rain that falls
slowly, playing against the leaves and touching water, rain but not
rain, a simple fountain giving droplets of water to the air,
the hovering trees, a pool at its feet where water echoes on the stone.
Everything seems to rest here, resting in the still fall
of water, an atom that contains a certain music, you, the stone

surrounding silence—time that seems to turn upon itself. You would
not dare to take a step for fear of altering the rhythms that
play upon the unknown world where you have strayed unable to
depart. Death is not noticed here, unless it is in inside the hollow
echo of the stones, of absence, sadness, a bird in darkness calling,
the notes barely heard and falling through your mind as any small
rain might fall, the traces that it leaves invisible but sure.

Last Apostrophe

Perhaps I shall see another spring, but if it is forbidden, I,
as I say farewell, will carry you in my heart, the you I loved as friends,
who will upon this last journey go with me into the light
or dark, as it may be, my heart carried by all of you to that
place where it must go, where flowers flower perhaps within the shade
of trees all new, but if fortune turns elsewhere, where darkness comes
and all the stars are gone, my one appeal will be for you, my love,

the you to whom these poems were given, the you that is the colour of
my voice, when nothing can be seen, my guide through all the eternities
we knew and shall, the you who gave to me the I that I became,
who in the dark will kneel and know that you are there beside me where
the dark is darkest. What other immortality can ever be
but this, to walk wherever your remembering eye is gazing, there
in that light that holds me still, all forever bound in us.

Sentinels

Like someone lying down beside an old church upon a summer
afternoon, head thrown back and gazing at the sky, the grass against
your hands so cool you might have thought a shower had quietly passed
somewhere though the air, and there were trees that stood around in such
a way that silence seemed to be what they exhaled, trees that were
as sentinels to ward against the coming of the dark—: in
the silence music barely audible was moving, music of birds
invisible but full of music that can only be the gift

of churches made of stone and wood and slow processions that move on
without end and disappear, only to return, to take
the shape of thought of all light. If you sleep, then memory
is where you lie, the memory that clings to old churches, so
serene you are but where lakes might come to rest, their surfaces
still in the pale light that spring bestows. No one can hear the least
reply of water, but everything stands attuned, sheathed in a skin of light,
the lakes barely breathing, music hesitant before it arrives.

Opened

It was a gate that opened soundlessly, inviting us to pass
inside and take our places but invisible and not known.
We knew that choice was left outside, that this was where we were to walk,
but where and for what purpose signs were not displayed, and so we walked
forward at first and soon from side to side, unsure as if we were
struck blind. I took your hand to know that you were there, and then we both
opened our eyes that we had merely closed, and then we knew that we

had never seen the world with open eyes, a world that there leaped up
with colours never seen by us before, and you cried out as if
you spoke a world in your throat, and such was the music that poured forth
that both us knew fear: perhaps that's all we were—music and
silence—gazing into colours that evoked a dream, a dream
that flowers, if they dream, might dream, but flowers that came out of air
like sudden showers, coming and going. Where had you gone, I thought, and so

to find you I stretched my hand toward the place where you had been: the dance
of flowers paused, roses hanging over me, and you were in
my eyes, nowhere else, a rose of infinite capacity
and nothing more, the rose of all the other roses, nothing left
for me to be but ground where you might stand where other roses might
surround you, each dancing again, no other knowledge given us
to understand what we might think things to be but such a dance.

Moonlight

Voices of children playing in the street rise up and float into
the window where you sit, the beauty of it seizing you as if
someone gripped your throat, your one desire to lift them in your arms,
embracing them forever, not the little bodies, which will grow old
soon enough, but just the voices, as elusive as a wild
stream that in the spring begins to stumble over rocks, and then
you think your heart will break, and unresisting that is what it does,

the fragments of it floating through the window and away from you
beyond your grasp, despite the empty gestures of your hands, appeals
of the mind in silence, mingling with the voices of the children,
silence, ostinatos they might hear perhaps to dance against,
among them yours and mine perhaps, a certain sadness that pervades
the light of afternoon, all that one desires most a gift
of bodies, bodies that shed their evanescence, a moonlight given up.

Surrendered

Before falling asleep at night, you curl your hand into a ball
and place it inside mine, and I, almost asleep, believe it is
a bird, my hand a nest, and for a moment the world seems to have
fallen asleep beside us, seas at rest upon their shores. How strange
it is, for all the creatures that are like us, falling into sleep
wherever they might be, surrendering themselves to something that
comes over them that they are in the dark about, something that
inhabits them and then departs to enter someone else, and takes

something of you bestowing it elsewhere, everyone become
as helpless as the smallest bird, and after years of sleeping like
a person sitting forever under rain. It is not possible
to know where all the rain has fallen, always flowing into one.
What belongs to you and me, so filled with sleep as we must be
that carries with it dreams that others must have dreamt, unable to
resist whatever happens to us, drifting through ourselves, possessed
of knowledge that seems to have gone off course, driftwood on a beach?

Weeping

Weeping is a music that is composed of oboes and the fine
rain that falls on distant hills, muted but with echoes of
poplar leaves that hold it briefly before giving it up, the sound
departure makes, unable to resist, an eternity
of going away that enters everything that hears it—seasons, chairs,
the moon—and standing in an old house, there's no running from
its rising from the walls, its dust invisible that settles on

your flesh without your feeling it. Weeping is a music that
exhales, coming over one as autumn mist that rises in
a valley, trees becoming ghosts, the ripple of the stream absorbed
but heard as weeping's only rhythm, breath the soul of weeping's cry,
the music that it makes drawn in, its waxing and its waning a
giving and a taking of the world, the stars that were so far
now brushing against our skin as if their sky had always been just there.

Heaven

Sometimes heaven simply lies down and sleeps in front of you.
You might have thought it paradise, but no, there's the limpid moon
and there the stars floating through it, and lying down, it eases into
a valley where in slow curves a river flows, and willows sweep
it in their silence, stars at your feet, a valley where nothing departs,
nocturnal birds in long ellipses passing and returning. Is this
where God sleeps, you ask, or is this heaven where God does not arrive,

and if there is no God here, what is this gift that's placed before
your feet, the music of the river barely rising to your ears,
the sleep that's nothing but complete surrender, birds that in the mind
of air turn upon themselves, a dance so intricate that none
can know its shapes, the air a tapestry asleep that none can see,
a heaven that is God but is God only given so,
and in it all you stand, breathing sleep, breathing the breath of God?

Beginning

The only place to start is where there seems to be nothing much
at all—a piece of paper where the words have not been written down,
a silence that has not occurred to music or a canvas that
has only known the colour white, an emptiness that you can feel
but not measure. God may have been there once, knowing the nothing that
hovered around him, waiting in some invisible idea that seemed
beyond any thought, like rain that hovers but never seems
to fall, a rain that has not been conceived, asleep in eternities

that have but one task, to wait, untroubled by a rain that has
not been called to fall, beneath a blank sky, waiting without
knowing for a single bird that steps into a garden where
nothing had been seen before, a bird that sings its single note,
a note recalling rain, a note that does not seem to be heard—
but you step out of it, a bird before you on a branch, and you
a bird and branch composing world enough, each belonging to
the same music, an air that gives you, back and forth, what you are.

Predestined

Often your voice is not much more than murmurs that flutter in
the dark like birds unsure of where they are, and then the murmur stops
in some nowhere only you have found. Even silence is
uncertain whether this is silence or a murmur not for us
to hear, and when you move, you move just as you speak, moving
somewhere you had not considered—: suddenly the world is
reshaped and given only to your eyes, the way a cat might move

to see the world at random and predestined, its shape the way you move,
and everything beside you knows that if the world is true, it will
rise inside your eyes exactly as it is, naked, fragile, and
on the point of disappearing, nothing held, the round
contours of all movement, movement moving round itself. The sun
goes down yet never the same way, its being without certainty,
and through its light children slip away, fates like toys in their hands.

Soror

When I heard that you had died, my eyes were resting on the sea,
an opalescent sea where the light like a child played, indifferent
to all that was around it, but drawing into it the light and birds
that hovered and were lifted up, disappearing into the sun,
and thinking of you, I was unable to turn my eyes away,
drawn like the birds into the sun and gone, only able to
recall you were for me the book that never opened, lying in

the darkness of the winter afternoons, no more than shadows of
things refusing to reveal themselves, amorphous shapes of trees,
houses perhaps along an unfamiliar street, and into that book
you had simply disappeared without the slightest sound, and should
I try to open it, the pages will be blank, the words in silence
gone away, like small animals that have no place to go,
moving into other winter afternoons that only they

are given leave to see. How to bid them farewell, to call into
the winter dark, not knowing where to look to see them pass? Perhaps
you are with them now, surrounding you with small sounds that you
will understand, leaving us in light beside the sea, allowed
to behold the play of it, the happiness of birds. When we were young,
I saw your face in profile near a window where the sun fell in.
How graceful was your hair where the light played. Your ringlets glistened, once.

Ghosts

And through the long winter afternoon after you had died,
we leafed through pictures spilling from their old boxes, gazing at
the faded faces of people some of us had known of or, at least,
had heard of, and stories rose into the dimming light, stories of you,
of mothers, fathers, children until several families floated in
the evening air, and we became surrounded by the ghosts of our
creation hovering over us, the tutelary deities
of our pasts, the we of all us, and gazing at each other

we began to see not merely us but shapes of all that we
had been. In such moments we are who we are but we as we
have never been before, the we that is never known until
we are brought into the long night that makes us who we are
and where, gazing on our faces over again, we see that there
is that place where the first stars emerge, the brilliance of it in
the room enough for all of us to give way, the ghostliness
of what we have summoned gone with us into the darkness and the light.

Grasped

When your spirit passed from us, a small smile appeared that I
had never seen before, hovering around the corners of
your mouth, as if what you had spent a lifetime searching for
arose before your eyes, and you took it in as something that
was always near but never seen, the hand, perhaps, that always without
the slightest touch guided you through the darkest dark, and here it was
again to take you in to the last dark and first light, and so

you know what flowers know, that all final things are first, between
them nothing to tell the first from the last, a flower holding light
and rain, the winds of night. If we are to rise where heaven might
be placed, we must, at that moment chosen for us, feel ourselves
open as new flowers, the emptiness we thought we might become
instantly overcome and now taken in hand, an unknown spring
moving through us, all night become the light it always was.

Boys

Father, I curse myself that when you lay upon your bed for the last
time, I should have taken you, helpless as you were, into
my arms and rocked you, as one might rock a fallen child, and sung you songs
as you had sung when you had been a boy, or told you all the stories
you told to me in my childhood so that the empty space
between the father and the child might have disappeared and in
its place nothing but a certain givingness would have taken

shape, a kind of garden where the light had no end, but where
the stars were always present, their light not overwhelmed by the sun,
and there you would have been carried, a burden so light you might
have thought you were already air—or I, neither of us knowing
who we were, like the moon new and old that carries itself
through the nights of the early month, both of us become a moon
of light and shade, hide and seek it might have been, among boys.

Swan Song

You rarely laughed, but when you spoke, the air around you seemed plumbed
anew, the birds against the windows each descending vertically
from the skies, the trees behind them straighter than before, and each
of them seemed called to where they were—not with one but with a host
of names, and all appeared to understand. If you had chanted Greek,
of Hector, say, laid out against his father's knees, the trees would have
trembled and begun to weep, and as if on strings the birds
in mid-flight would have hung in flocks from clouds. But you were not
alone, Roy yet rather Rex, king of a domain that spread

through pages of infinities of words, each one a star that had
fallen from galaxies to mark the bright landscape where you walked,
talking with all of them as intimates, a kind of happiness
sifting through the air, a king whose only peers could be the stars,
and if they spoke to you, apotheosis must have been assumed.
How many summers passed so, their undisturbed descent a rain
so gentle it could have come and gone with no one knowing if it had
come at all, nothing more than flowers nodding their replies.

And then, after many a summer, the barge that came for you paused
against the shores of that lake that stretched beyond the edge of your
domain, a barge where you must lie, a barge that carries you to that
farther domain where the order of the stars takes its origin,
and birds, and trees that always were more anagogic than they seemed.
Hardly a sound it makes, hardly a wake, the passage of it all
that's needed, as silent as a script in languages unknown and never
seen before, mysterious joy, a bird singing, the night revealed.

Encompassed

You may have wondered why, in late afternoon, a few clouds
appeared against the sky, clouds that were not there at sunrise, clouds
that moved slowly toward the far horizon, everyone gazing at
them, taken by a kind of silence falling like rain, some
of the clouds so small they seem like birds that hover near before they head
for home, clouds of uncertainty, then, that move and do not move, but wait
for wind, for night, for anything that might ruffle the undisturbed

sky. Crystal in certain lights carries such clouds, and as
you gaze into it, the sky is not the skin transparent of
a universe, but all its depth displays itself for you, of light
refracting everywhere, and turning you see it before you and behind—:
where can you be if not inside the crystal of the sky, the sea
encompassing itself, and falling forever on every shore it knows,
lying still against your feet, the future of the flower already

passed again, and still coming round, all its passages
contained within itself, the clouds you saw before you now encircling
you and themselves, homing birds always at home. How to tell
the light of afternoon from morning? Perhaps we imagine stars we think
are always coming and going, the stars that give the sky eternity,
floating out across the sea. They rise at our feet. How easy it is
to kneel beside them, or walk from one and then another, returned.

Bowl

All the little artefacts that speak of what a life has been,
beginning, perhaps, with children, their quick cries that make the bright air
yet brighter before darkness falls, things that stand behind glass,
things cut from glass, shaped from porcelain, a wooden bowl
that you loved to hold at certain times of day, to wonder at
the air invisible inside it, an air there but only for itself
and yet for you, as if a world beyond sight was lying there
that made you who were, a wooden bowl, the quiet air, and hands

that held it all in silence that no one can fathom. It's possible
a sea undiscovered lay there, dry with all its fossils
still intact, patterns of ferns, dreams of fish—: why is this
enough to bring you to the edge of softly weeping, everything
surrounding you now disappeared, all that is left a wooden bowl,
your hands assuming its shape and you inside among the ferns that are
unable to be seen, a bowl that has been passed from God's hands
into yours, not knowing what more to do with it than holding it so.

Abiding

Trying to follow the drift of your mind growing slowly younger as
your hands unnoticed grow softer, how you turn to follow a bird's path,
absorbed by certain measures of music or words in the language that you spoke
when young, trying to fathom a world that is without the slightest measure,
taking the summer of flowers in with well-remembered care, perhaps
an afternoon for single roses, full of awe as suns go down
over the bay, all your beliefs unshaken still and held in that

place where all the suns undisturbed still turn, no threnody
but theirs avails where, if the most ancient of light is traceable,
it abides, or in the first flower. What other drift does your mind
follow, there where love does not grow but infinitesimally
expands, the moment after the voices of singing children fall silent,
but not a moment, rather an age where ice returns and disappears,
or single stars that flower, filling the night, until another appears?

Flowering

You may have thought that dying was an end, all the doors closed,
the windows of the morning fallen, and the sun that had come up
faithfully in your flesh, flashing through the streams of spring, the lake
that could be nothing but forever, the sky spread upon it night
and day—all of it put out, and the stars, all the light
become a crow that sings what holds the universe together, all
the visible mere mirage. How to wake, what air to breathe,
and how to spell it now, nothing to see and nothing to hide, shade

consuming all. But never more than earth we were, dear friend, if earth
infinitesimal, the one gift that we were given to speak,
saying what we knew as prayers counting the hours of the night,
your mouth spilling over with the yellow immortelles and
the silence that is in them filling all the air we breathe, the small
suns that are beyond all dark a light that we can lift,
our hands spilling over with the earth. How can we speak of dark,
of dark where light in its eternity flows upon our flesh?

Unfolding

We looked at one another—slowly, like water that moves along
a creek when it has flowed from that time when all the ice withdrew,
a water that was all that water was and was meant to be,
water that had passed directly from the hand of God to this
forgotten creek to trickle slowly toward the sea as if it were
how being comes into sight and disappears. We did not speak,
but simply gazed and saw the colour of our eyes, and how the light

arose, the only necessary sun, and what stars might find
residence between them, all other suns and stars slipping
away as if they had never been, their certainties eclipsed.
We looked at one another—this must be how all creatures sleep,
completely given up, sunk into the shape a creek will make
as it flows into its own forever where the sea lies,
all things remembered in their fullness, the ice and the thaw.

Echoed

As you lie down beside me, a draft of air rises slowly over—
over all that falls beneath its compass—like breezes that in spring
after rain passing quickly overhead, a light that flashes through
poplar leaves, such a breeze that rises up like stars through mist,
the shapes of things unclear, but all brought knowing into the light,
almost waking, still asleep, looking neither forward nor back,
knowing this is how eternity comes down, something that trees

know already in their seeds, but we without sleep, without
the helplessness that leads us there, cannot be brought to feel so,
the everywhere peopled by the stars flowing over your hands,
everything become its own breathing nakedly exposed
to all breathing, the only coming and only going, no singing
left but of this, the great music unheard, yet echoes lying down
beside us, taking our breath away and then coming back with it.

Star

You and I were lying where willows and their leaves spread over
us and lakes of still waters, murmuring music to our ears,
a music not of birds but of unknown animals with large
eyes that wander through the twilight of their forests searching for
the moon, and everything we thought we knew fell away from us
like rain departing, the air remaining, softly lit and fresh as if
morning stood alone inside us, waiting to be seen, the moon

still alive and late stars. Nothing called out, no birds
or dogs that lost their way, but something whispered through us barely to
be heard, no more than echoes as of shells that open in the light,
or shells that merely think of light before returning to the night,
perhaps the light itself, its opening invisible, its music not
heard but known when gone, its presence and its absence all it gives,
the morning that is ours the breath that lies upon the farthest star.

Apple Trees

You were not beside me on that day when walking into town
I saw that all was now no longer what it was when we would walk
this way. I thought at first it was the houses that had somehow changed,
the apple trees that had been standing near and now were not, the birds
that were no longer singing in the trees that were not there, the stream
that trickled out of sight. How quickly I forgot that all of this
must have passed without my taking thought, and when it did, it did
not seem to matter, given no more thought than taking a breath or
walking through a door, but when it is noticed, it becomes a sign

of what is there and was not there before, grasping at what is not
for any one to grasp. What Sunday of the mind is made to hold
the light invisible that is around us but unable to
bring before our unaccustomed eyes the order bells might bring
and spires against horizons keeping clouds in place. If you were now
beside me, we would see that what we could not see at all before
us, and where the apple trees no longer stand is where you and I
might stand if we were standing underneath their branches bright with flowers,
the sun falling past the spires toward the stream out of sight.

Waiting Again

Walking through the slow silence of your eyes, unable to
know now when light begins or how the darkness forms, or where
the mountains stand infinite against the shore. Turning back is not
a possibility, the shape of waiting falling, leaves the nearest
contour to assume, their stillness in the sun, the wind that breathes
upon them hardly greater than the moon, a drawing inward where
we are asked to take place, the ceremony that you thought
would circulate around us present but not seen, a kind of murmur,

the choreography forgotten but the master of the place
impromptu, not a dance for feet but something yet to be named,
calling out without a sound, and followed as one follows music
never heard before, and there the great giving arrives, the trees
you thought you saw each a portal open to the waiting that each
leaf exhales, the waiting that no one can fail to draw in,
prayer put aside, even the sun its great fires taking
waiting in to give it back, each planet waiting to turn.

Sky

You said it was the trees that gave the sky the beauty it possessed,
the same sky that lies across the lakes, the trees growing down,
but down into the sky where fish find their way among the leaves,
a flash of light that disappears. And so we are, almost always,
inside the sky, our shadows sometimes almost reaching it, where they
become infinitesimal clouds dissolving in the sun. But when
darkness obscures the trees, the leaves, and fish, we become a sky
that is each other's sky, neither mine nor yours, but still a sky

that rises from each other's eyes, a sky that holds its own clouds,
its own trees and lakes, a sky that has been always ours, and more
deeply placed inside the sky given to everyone, and once perceived,
rising as if inevitably above the known stars that we
are given, each marking its own heaven that rise as slow autumn
mornings almost hidden in the mist, the air around us clear
and heavy with still light floating between us back and forth, our eyes
incapable of other things to see, the light mere breath.

Dissolution

In that eternity that is the way our childhood is brought
to mind yours appears where you are lying at one with mysterious grass
that rises into bells of flowers ringing mutely in the air
swollen with summer and birds that pass in sudden flutters, the business
of smaller creatures. How peacefully dissolution flows through your mind
falling asleep, the world at rest with itself, the bees weaving air.
This is the time you were given, the rhythm holding you in what   .
you seem to be, but from you flows the longer pace where trees spring up,

and all that holds the centre and forgotten stars, the great curves
that keep the planets in their arcs, the guides invisible and still,
and when you lie now, the memory of bees turning in
the air, there is no past that comes to mind but you in what you are
where flowers have their being, that enormous silence that rests inside
the rose, undying summers of undying grass where you, the sun
and rolling auroras move in the same flux, the questions one might ask
answered by the same unfolding and folding again, gladness asleep.

Echoing

If anything resembles you, it is a feline presence that
settles over you like shades that gather under tall trees
yielding to the slight air and moving without contrariety
wherever winds choose to move, without a sense of north and so
light they are that everything appears inside them as if it were
silence always embodied, partly itself and partly something else,
hardly empty, a silence shaped, stillness possessed, a silence that
is born after music falls, before an echo arrives. It is

the silence waiting where the road begins to turn that may have lain
lurking unnumbered years before anyone arrives, as old
as sky, the being of the place and waiting to be seen, the shape
it takes unwinding from eternity and always close to slipping
away, and all that opens on the way, the trees, the rippling leaves
leap up in echo of what spreads behind, silence figured there,
its music now remembered, the quick shades of what it was complete,
moving around in measured gravity, the moon unfolding again.

Seeking

There is no flower that you do not stop for, no leaf unworthy of
another look, no colour that does not provide a red or green
unseen before, but all of them, all the gardens that you pass
begin to grow in memory where other flowers you have known
take root again and lift into that space where you are called
to be and all the knowledge that possesses you takes you again
into its leafy hands, the grass beneath your feet more at home
in you than any dream, the child that you were and constantly

run towards to see runs away just beyond your hands,
the you that you believe you are a child free among the lanes
of flowers, each drawing you, the child you wish to be into
the flower that you are, but such a flower that cannot be still
like other flowers in the ground, the grass unmoving next to them,
all of them at home where they spring up, and so with arms outstretched
you make your way through the world, another world where the petals
that you are all open to gather them into your light.

Polaris

Certain that whatever truth there might be it lay among
the stars, and so we dreamed that when we were far apart, we
would chose one star where our eyes in darkness would meet, a star
unlike other stars that held without our knowing either gods
or fate, and there, our vision never so clear, our eyes would be conjoined,
held by a star, as if no other wisdom but the wisdom of
a child, wise with innocence, could place us in a universe,
where solar winds and passing meteors were for a moment stilled,

but what no child could have said was that we did not meet in dark—:
light it was that overcame us, a light that flowed from a single star
and entered us where blood used to flow, rivulets of light
that next to them drew in their own birds and flowers that did not
fail but their uncertain spring danced and danced and spring became
perpetual, the only truth that need embrace the world, where our
eyes have met, unable other light to know, where night is not
the night but merely light barely awake, dreaming of the dawn.

Childhood

Sometimes I wonder if you saw anything other than the shades
of green while gazing over fields toward the sea, shades of green
melting into farther blue, and if someone were standing in
the fields, what shade they might be, and how their colours might change
were they to move outside the light, or if a flock of birds began
descending from the sea to seek what they might eat before the dark
envelops them, the shades of what they were become invisible,
absorbed into the fields and sea, but you, where were you, what shade

was yours, when darkness overcame the air, what colour was your sleep
beneath the deep silence of the passing birds, the sea passing up
and down the coast against the fields, and what colour was the great
silence filling the sea, and after you were gone into that dark
that no one remembers, how was I to know what shade was yours, when you
were never present in the vast fields but merely casting an air
without silence over all you saw, and shades and something that
dispelled time, and nothing, not even you, holding the slightest breath?

Undecided

Undecided, you were standing on the steps descending from
an old cathedral, the great portals behind you closed, gazing where
the early light was spilling into a square, the awkward pigeons near
your feet growing warm. And so you were, many years ago,
the brightness in your eyes unforgotten. How much it says, your hand
brushing mine in this place where we, no cathedrals in sight,
sit, the light changed, the pigeons still as awkward. Is it you,
the you that you remember in the square, who did descend the steps

to disappear in morning light, the you you want to be again,
or is it now no more than what you dream of, wanting all the squares
to come to one place where you stand still, all that you have been
fresh and full of early light, and not believing that the light is how
you came to be and what you are, the light you think that you see through
is what contains all the you you are, remembering you before
you were without the need for pigeons and cathedrals, nothing lost,
the light without which blindness would have been mine, astray in a dark wood?

Epilogue

Now that death has finally entered me, I must bid you farewell,
my love, a word I never wished to speak to you, never fitting
how we spoke, and so I must go forward slowly, searching bit
by bit what path in this dark wood to take, but in a forest old
and well travelled. I think of the poets who could not see
the barest difference between love and death, too short-lived
to know that love, the truest wife of life, rises like a slow
moon, to rest above the heart disarming death, its light breathless

and serene. That is the light that speaks to us and then enters us
when first mine and then your heart will break, mine collapsing
but yours barely opening where mine is taken into yours
leaving a scarcely visible line, the seal where you and I become
the we we will remain until time ends, our heads always at rest
one leaning upon the other, our eyes gazing into who
we are, and when you speak, your breath and mine will rise and fall
as our breath, and what you say only saying us, where

the wood, its darkness given up, spreads out in flowers beneath the moon
carrying your words into its light. Walking is easy here, gentle
as the phasing moon, drawing in and then letting its breath
go, teaching the heart in its hours moving through open air,
flowers alone beneath its feet. All the silence it creates
is ours, all the music rising and falling from its pace is ours,
your heart slowly rocking mine beneath the lullaby the moon
makes, all the light only ours, our our ours.

31 March 2018 (Easter Eve)

Other Titles by E.D. Blodgett
from University of Alberta Press

Songs for Dead Children

Timeless and powerful poems
contemplating eternity, grief and love
in a reflective and quiet way.

as if

Visceral musings explore the intertwining
connection between the human and the
natural worlds.

Apostrophes VII
Sleep, You, a Tree

Sumptuous imagery, commanded by
musical lines and understated language,
reveals the poet's breathtaking vision.

More information at uap.ualberta.ca